# Testimonials

I0567480

This book left me with a smile and feeling encouraged. Not to mention the useful tools throughout all the chapters. I have rolled with life's highs and lows, building myself up and picking myself back up again and again. Only to be discouraged about starting all over again. but after reading Chapter 10, "Turning a Crisis into Abundance." I feel like a breath of fresh air has blown in, bringing new life to starting over and eliminating unnecessary stress. In Chapter 2, Lisa's HHG, is a kind reminder to listen to your Head, Heart, and Gut.

I'm envisioning hugging myself when I find myself in a challenging situation. HHG: check in with head, heart and utilize my gut instinct. I've found when I've questioned my gut instinct or gone against it, the results are not the best. Being gently reminded to HHG is a great gift to oneself. This is a wonderful book, written by two highly knowledgeable experienced coaches. I encourage all my friends to read this book; it's a great resource to have at your fingertips. **Dani Davis**

I loved this book!! The guidance and care can be felt in each chapter. There are so many nuggets of information and so many helpful tools for my toolbox, that it's hard for me to focus on one thing. Reminders of self-care and building the relationships in your life that fulfill your soul in all areas of your life. Jesse and Lisa hit it out of the park with this book.

As I was reading it I found I had lost sight of the center elements of my life that brought me joy and now I will go back through the book for self-reflection to make the changes I need to make to bring that joy back into my life. I will explore myself and then move to my relationships to make improvements, with accountability and a new plan using this book as my guide. This book brought me a renewed sense of how I want to see my future and recommit to myself, marriage, family, and friends!! **Christy Bouhourdin**

# HOW YOU LEAVE THEM FEELING

*Your Foundation for Inspiring Relationships*
*Interactive Companion Workbook*

By

## Lisa Ferrell & Jesse Ferrell

How You Leave Them Feeling: Your Foundation for Inspiring Relationships - Interactive Companion Workbook © Copyright 2024 Lisa Ferrell & Jesse Ferrell

For more information, email lisalisten9@jesstalk.com

ISBN: 979-8-89316-777-1 - Paperback
ISBN: 979-8-89316-776-4 - Ebook

# How You Leave Them Feeling
# Your Foundation for Inspiring Relationships

## INTERACTIVE COMPANION WORKBOOK

Lisa Ferrell and Jesse Ferrell are International Speakers, Master Coaches & Award-winning Authors. JessTalk Speaking & Coaching Firm was founded in 2001 with a powerful mission to help free others from their concerns by connecting through a context of love & joy.

Jesse and Lisa created this workbook to provide a structured system for completing the exercises in their book, *How You Leave Them Feeling: Your Foundation for Inspiring Relationships.*

### INTERACTIVE COMPANION WORKBOOK OPENING VIDEO
### Scan the QR code below to get started

# Chapters Table of Contents

# Interactive Table of Contents

## CHAPTER 1

# Living Life by Design

Living life by design means taking the time to develop and create the important areas of your life. It happens when you refuse to take the easy way. You refuse to stand by and wait to see what life may or may not bring you.

Happenstance is when you live your life hoping to *get lucky*—meet the person of your dreams, land your supreme job, career path, or entrepreneurial business of a lifetime. Typically, happenstance occurs without your awareness. So many of us have lived and can relate to living by happenstance. It occurs when you allow things to happen *to you* without taking any agency over them.

The following exercise will help you understand who you are, what matters to you, and how you can intentionally design your life instead of living it by happenstance. To receive your best growth and development, **please answer the questions on the following page with vulnerability and honesty.**

1

## Exercise 1

What do you want for and from your life?

_____

_____

_____

_____

_____

_____

_____

_____

_____

_____

_____

_____

Who are the people in your circle of influence that will help you grow and develop and hold you accountable?

_____

_____

_____

_____

_____

_____

# What Matters Most Roles Assessment

In understanding what matters most to you, it is important to become present with the various roles you play in your life. Below are examples of the various roles you may play. Circle or add the ones relevant to you.

| | |
|---|---|
| Parent | Volunteer |
| Child | Coach |
| Sibling | Teammate |
| Friend | Listener |
| Spouse/Partner | Leader |
| Employee/Worker | Follower |
| Boss/Manager | Citizen |
| Business Owner | Neighbor |
| Student | Customer/Client |
| Teacher/Mentor | Consumer |
| Caregiver | Advocate/Activist |

**Add roles you play that aren't listed above.**

_____     _____

_____     _____

_____     _____

_____     _____

# What Matters Most Values Assessment

**Below are examples of the various values you may have in your life. Circle or add the ones that are relevant to you.**

| | |
|---|---|
| Family/Friends | Compassion |
| Health | Integrity |
| Spirituality/God/Religion | Trust |
| Time | Gratitude |
| Intuition | Respect |
| Goals | Forgiveness |
| Love | Passion |
| Education | Creativity |
| Career | Adventure |
| Financial stability | Purpose |
| Happiness | Freedom |
| Kindness | Inner peace |

**Add values you have that aren't listed above.**

_____     _____

_____     _____

_____     _____

_____     _____

# 5-Star What Matters Most Assessment – Roles Phase I

1. List your ten most important roles in your portfolio below, examples of roles: father, husband, brother, sister, business owner, educator, etc.

2. Using a 5-Star rating system, rate your roles' importance to you (5 = very important and 1 = least important).

3. Rate the performance of how well you are living into each of your roles below (5 = highest level of living in your roles and 1 = lowest level of living in your roles). See the example on the following page.

## 5–Star What Matters Most Portfolio Phase I

| Count | Importance Level (0-5 stars) | Individual Roles | Performance Rating (0-5 stars) |
|---|---|---|---|
| 1 | | | |
| 2 | | | |
| 3 | | | |
| 4 | | | |
| 5 | | | |
| 6 | | | |
| 7 | | | |
| 8 | | | |
| 9 | | | |
| 10 | | | |

## 5-Star What Matters Most Portfolio Phase I Example

| Count | Importance Level (0-5 stars) | Individual Roles | Performance Rating (0-5 stars) |
|---|---|---|---|
| 1 | 4.0 | Educator | 4.0 |
| 2 | 4.0 | Leader | 3.0 |
| 3 | 4.0 | Friend | 3.5 |
| 4 | 5.0 | Wife | 4.0 |
| 5 | 5.0 | Partner | 3.0 |
| 6 | 4.0 | Peacemaker | 3.0 |
| 7 | 4.0 | Role Model | 4.0 |
| 8 | 5.0 | Relationship Manager | 3.5 |
| 9 | 5.0 | Problem Solver | 3.0 |
| 10 | 4.5 | Business Owner | 3.5 |
|  | 4.5 |  | 3.5 |

In Chapter 5: The Relationship Excellence Suite, we will revisit your 5-Star What Matters Most Portfolio.

## 5-Star What Matters Most Assessment – Values Phase II

1. List your ten most important governing values in your Governing Values Profile below.

2. Using a 5-star rating system, rate your values' importance to you
   (5 = very important and 1 = least important).

3. Rate the performance of how well you are living into each of your values.
   (5 = highest level of living into your values and 1 = lowest level of living into your roles).

4. Briefly describe why your values are important to you in the 5-Star What Matters Most Governing Values Profile. See the example on the following page.

# 5–Star What Matters Most Governing Values Profile

| Count | Individual Governing Values | Value Rating | Performance Rating | My Governing Values Statements & Why They Are Important To Me |
|-------|------------------------------|--------------|--------------------|---------------------------------------------------------------|
| 1 | | | | |
| 2 | | | | |
| 3 | | | | |
| 4 | | | | |
| 5 | | | | |
| 6 | | | | |
| 7 | | | | |
| 8 | | | | |
| 9 | | | | |
| 10 | | | | |
| | | | | |

# 5 – Star What Matters Most Governing Values Profile Example

| Count | Individual Governing Values | Value Rating | Performance Rating | My Governing Values Statements & Why They Are Important To Me |
|-------|------------------------------|--------------|--------------------|---------------------------------------------------------------|
| 1 | Mental Health | 5.0 | 4.0 | Being mentally healthy allows me to have the proper mindset to work through or resolve all life matters in a good spirit. |
| 2 | Physical Health | 5.0 | 4.0 | Maintaining good physical health gives me positive energy to live out a full range of nonconstricting life choices. |
| 3 | Love | 5.0 | 4.5 | Love is one of the deepest, most positive emotions that touches us in many ways. |
| 4 | Faithfulness | 5.0 | 5.0 | Faithfulness demonstrates your desire to be respectful and truthful to those with whom you have relationship agreements. |
| 5 | Honesty | 5.0 | 4.5 | Honesty allows others to build trust and offers communication and intention that they count on. |
| 6 | The Power of Words | 5.0 | 4.0 | Respecting the power of words puts me in the driver's seat, allowing me to leave people and situations better than I found them. |
| 7 | Peace of Mind | 5.0 | 4.0 | Good peace of mind allows me to live peacefully in my skin. |
| 8 | Personal Responsibility | 4.0 | 4.0 | Personal responsibility is a measure of taking full ownership while remaining accountable. |
| 9 | Intuition | 4.0 | 3.5 | Tapping into intuition allows me to connect with my inner guiding system, using instincts and my gut to guide me. |
| 10 | Time (value & usage of time) | 5.0 | 4.5 | Time is the most precious commodity; it's perishable but invaluable. I honor, respect, and use it wisely. |
| | | 4.8 | 4.2 | |

7

**What is your WHY?**

Search inside yourself and determine your biggest WHY in your life plan. (Don't worry if you don't know your WHY just yet. We are about to walk you through an exercise to develop it.)

**Why do you want to pursue the lifestyle you are choosing?**

_____

_____

_____

_____

_____

**Get on Track by Developing Your Why**

Our BOST process will help you understand what you want from each area of your life and how to create a plan to achieve it. As always, answer honestly.

# BOST: Background - Objective - Strategy - Tactics

**Background**—Start your plan by writing a description of the key personal and professional areas of growth and achievement that have allowed you to gain success up to your current place in life.

**How has each personal and professional growth and achievement area shaped your journey?**

_____

_____

_____

_____

_____

**Objective** -Write your clarifying objective.

**What specific steps will you outline in your clarifying objective to propel your growth and development to the next level?**

_____

_____

_____

_____

_____

_____

_____

_____

_____

_____

_____

_____

_____

_____

_____

_____

_____

_____

_____

_____

_____

_____

**Strategy** - Create a written strategy for prioritizing critical areas of your life to identify what is most important to you. Here are some of the vital areas:

**Family**

_____

_____

_____

_____

_____

_____

_____

**Health**

_____

_____

_____

_____

_____

_____

**Professional Development**

_____

_____

_____

_____

_____

_____

**Relationships (intimate, friends, colleagues)**

**Education**

**Goals**

Next, you must establish the importance of each key area, as they are likely connected. For example, you may find professional development very important. Still, if you fail to save time and space for managing your health and family, you may negatively impact these key areas.

Managing these BOST components will help you as needed in meaningful areas of your life.

**Tactics** - Design clear, definable, and measurable processes to ensure the actions you take are in complete alignment with your Objectives.

_____

_____

_____

_____

_____

_____

**Strengths & Weaknesses** - Include your strengths and weaknesses and share what you are good at and where you need to improve. If you aren't sure of what your strengths and weaknesses are, be willing to ask a few people who know you well and with whom you have an excellent relationship. They may see things, talents, or areas of needed improvement that you can't see in yourself.

**Strengths**

_____

_____

_____

_____

_____

**Weaknesses**

_____

_____

_____

_____

_____

**Goals** - What are the top three goals you want to accomplish during your lifetime? Take another close look at your why, objective, strategy, values, and roles to help guide your creation and map out your goals. You may want to write your goals down in different categories.

Some examples of varying goal categories may include the following:

**Health** - It's crucial to prioritize your health by scheduling regular check-ups with a doctor or health professional.

_____

_____

_____

_____

_____

**Personal** - Travel to Europe and visit Italy, France, Croatia, and Spain.

_____

_____

_____

_____

_____

_____

**Spiritual** - A sense of conviction that a more significant connection exists beyond the self, linking us all together.

_____

_____

_____

_____

**Physical** - Being physically active, weight management, daily stretching, and workouts.

_____

_____

_____

_____

_____

**Professional** - Strive for excellence in your field of study, increase your earnings.

_____

_____

_____

_____

_____

_____

Once you have written out your goals, the next step is to determine how you will accomplish them. Take an honest and clear assessment of where you stand right now. This will help determine what steps you need to take to reach your goals and fully live into your life plan.

Creating your life plan is a precursor to the roadmap. It helps you live your best life and adjust as needed. Review your plan weekly and record your accomplishments and growth every month.

Remember that your life plan is a fluid process and ever-changing.

*"Setting Goals is The First Step in Turning the Invisible into the Visible." Tony Robbins*

# Crafting Your Life Plan

A solid structure for building your life plan will include the following components:

1. 5-Year Outlook (long-term vision)
2. 3-Year Perspective (mid-term vision)
3. 1-Year View
4. 90-Day Plan (personal and professional)
5. Life Plan Benefits

Below is an example of a completed life plan.

## My 5-Year Outlook Life Plan

| Value | Goal | Why These Goals Are Important | What Kind of Person Must I Become to Reach Goal | Strategy |
|---|---|---|---|---|
| 5 | Change others life by my presence | Ability to help more people in a time efficient fashion | Must continue to be patient with others | Must always continue to be patient with others |
| 4 | Dramatically improve societies | To become a global presence | Must become and remain a learned and studied person | Gain connections with global leaders |
| 4 | Find a way to help make life complete for my parents | To repay the gift of life | Be available and increase my exposure to both of them | Start by blocking weekend visits now |
| 4 | Set many new paradigms in creative thinking | To help bring about positive change | I must remain clear and focused, surrounded by other positive lights | Block time for silence and thinking moments daily |
| 4.5 | Become financially independent | To serve self and others at the highest levels | Open for growth and learning financial intelligence and connect with the best financial advisors | Leave our financial advisor and hire a new intelligent advisor that cares |

| 4.3 | Average Value Rating |
|---|---|

| | Value Legend |
|---|---|
| 5 | Highest Value and Impact |
| 4 | High Value and Impact |
| 3 | Important Value and Impact |
| 2 | Modestly Valuable |
| 1 | Significant |

## My 3-Year Outlook Life Plan

| Value | Goal | Why These Goals Are Important | What Kind of Person Must I Become to Reach Goal | Strategy |
|---|---|---|---|---|
| 5 | Become a person of great influence | Allowing others to help make my life better and use my best talents to improve their lives | Ask higher powers for the direction and path to follow | Look for powerful people to welcome into my village |
| 5 | Remain well-spoken, educated, healthy, strong and energetic | This helps to demonstrate the making of a legend | Someone who shares the best modeling concepts | Search for role models and examples of excellent character |
| 5 | Redefine leadership | There is no reason we have to keep the same archetypes | I must learn from the masters while creating a new model | Attend leadership conferences and read the leadership books |
| 4 | Payback our clients 100-fold | Pay it forward program | Remain open to support all people and discover the best resources to share and serve others | Never forget the power of my global village |
| 4 | Learn to write effectively and passionately | Writing effectively and passionately allows me to communicate effectively, reaching a broad range of audiences | I must write from the heart | Write a minimum of one hour per day, every day |

| 4.6 | Average Value Rating |
|---|---|

| | Value Legend |
|---|---|
| 5 | Highest Value and Impact |
| 4 | High Value and Impact |
| 3 | Important Value and Impact |
| 2 | Modestly Valuable |
| 1 | Significant |

## My 1-Year View

| Value | Goal | Why These Goals Are Important | What Kind of Person Must I Become to Reach Goal | Strategy |
|---|---|---|---|---|
| 5 | We maintain a healthy body, mind, and spirit | To create a bio-balanced state of being | One who seeks continual improvement | We share health meetings every Sunday |
| 5 | We resonate at positive energy levels | This energy is therapeutic to all others, even with no direct conversation with them | This supports us seeking to help many people | Check with our accountability partners how our energy resonates |
| 4 | We consistently lead leaders | To assure our talents and abilities are appreciated and stimulated | Strong, consistent, clear, and concise communicators | We practice strengthening our communication muscles daily |
| 4 | We help our family live their best lives now | To assist them with living happy & healthy lives | Ready to help whenever they are ready to grow and learn | Remain open for the opportunity to serve others |
| 4 | We write creatively, affectionately, effectively, and passionately | To reach other audiences who may be helped by our writings | Continue the practice of writing and securing help to improve | Maintain this as a daily practice |

| 4.4 | Average Value Rating |
|---|---|

| | Value Legend |
|---|---|
| 5 | Highest Value and Impact |
| 4 | High Value and Impact |
| 3 | Important Value and Impact |
| 2 | Modestly Valuable |
| 1 | Significant |

## My 90-Day Plan

| AREAS | 90-Day Plan |
|---|---|
| Area #1 | Health & Wellness Plan |
| 1 | I am meditating for 21 days for the Oprah - Deepak Chopra relationship challenge. |
| 2 | I am reading to understand and know all 7 Chakras and how they work. |
| 3 | I am working out and getting the proper daily rest to insure optimum health, wellness, favor, grace and peace. |
| 4 | I am attending yoga 1-2 times per week and schedule it with Christy. |
| 5 | I am scheduling a family dinner once a month. |
| 6 | I am continuing to eat 3 healthy meals per day 6 days per week in order to achieve my goal weight of 125 lbs in 8 months. |
| 7 | I am educating myself by reading Dr. Jon Barron's book recommended by Paul Grady. |
| 8 | I am reading 1 hour per day in order to get into Ayurvedic alignment, as well as living the lifestyle for my type of food to eat. |
| Area #2 | Personal & Professional Development Plan |
| 1 | I surround myself with top executives and like-minded individuals (the information exchange develops my full self). |
| 2 | I invest 2 hours per day in business development (coaching, networking, and structural redevelopment) 5 days per week. |
| 3 | I am building Conversations into a paid platform and new product development through JessTalk & LisaListen. |
| 4 | I am committed to the What Matters Most program and submitting to 3 success coaching sessions per month. |
| 5 | I am mastering my elevator speech and will have it fully developed and memorized by the end of the month. |
| 6 | I am networking and researching with coaches at least twice per month to continue to develop my business and coaching style. |
| 7 | I am committed to writing in my journal 15 minutes 4 days per week. |
| 8 | I am developing my life vision for health, professional life, finances and travel. |
| Area #3 | Financial Development Plan |
| 1 | My goal of reaching financial independence is supported by my financial freedom objectives and I review daily with my partner. |
| 2 | I am continuing my path to financial intelligence, budgeting, reading, and paying attention to the law and energy of money. |
| 3 | I am reviewing our Cash Flow Statement monthly with Robert Lee & Associates Accounting Firm. |
| 4 | I am disciplined to collaborate with and review weekly our Cash Flow Statement with my partner. |
| 5 | I am reading a minimum of one financial intelligence book per month. |
| 6 | My credit card balances are kept to a zero balance and paid off weekly. |
| 7 | I have made a commitment to pay myself first (20% of my gross earnings) every month. |
| 8 | I maintain positive growth in my bank accounts. |
| 9 | I am focused on building multiple streams of additional income. |

## My Life Plan Benefits

| | |
|---|---|
| 1 | Master Organizational System - designed for achieving life goals & development |
| 2 | Shifting Priorities - Rank and priority system allowing you to manage a world of shifting priorities |
| 3 | Creative Thinking - Dedicated use of this life plan adds a major assist in clearing your mind and adds accountability |
| 4 | Set The Table - My life plan is constantly showing me personal & professional growth |
| 5 | Targets & deadlines - My life plan helps me stay focused on my targets & deadlines |

Use the examples provided on the previous pages of this chapter starting from your 5-Year Outlook Life Plan down to My 90-Day Plan. Scan the QR Code below to download My Life Plan example and a blank copy for your use.

## Living Your Life by Design

The best way to improve the odds of living your life by design is to find an accountability partner you love and trust. Create an agreement with your accountability partner that their number one role is to hold your feet to the fire and not let you off the hook regarding staying the course throughout your entire plan.

You are likely living your life through the false limiting beliefs you were taught early on. One example of a false limiting belief would be the idea that to get a good job and make a lot of money, you have to get good grades in high school so that you can go to college. Then, you must graduate from college and get a good job for 25 - 35 years, look forward to retirement from ages 62 - 67, and do nothing during your retirement years.

We call this predominantly taught standard of life the *old* form of getting ready, or what we call the old GRASP. **GRASP stands for Getting Ready, Attitude, Signature, and Passion.**

We are not submitting scientific evidence that retiring and doing nothing equates to death. However, in our experience over our fifty-five years of serving and witnessing countless lives, we have seen those following the old GRASP concept die within six years of retiring. We have found that structure and purpose are key to living a longer and more fulfilled life, yet so many people don't have a positive retirement plan.

These old GRASP attitudes are focused on a tired and worn-out form of the ideal life. In mindsets like this, one doesn't focus on building their brand, what we call our "signature." Without consistently adjusting an attractive and positive attitude supported by the knowledge of our unique signature, one has no passion for life beyond the old GRASP life concept.

We believe that following the old GRASP model puts you in the front seat for living a life of happenstance. See a snapshot of what the old GRASP looks like below.

## The Old GRASP

To avoid the old GRASP trap, we recommend adopting and adapting to the new form of GRASP. The new form of GRASP is simply choosing to live your life by design!

By adopting the new form of GRASP, you move beyond the common life roadmap and focus beyond getting good grades during your early Getting Ready stages of life.

You become intentional about upgrading your attitude and discovering an opportunity to continue improving your signature and live your life passionately. See a snapshot of the new GRASP below.

## The New GRASP

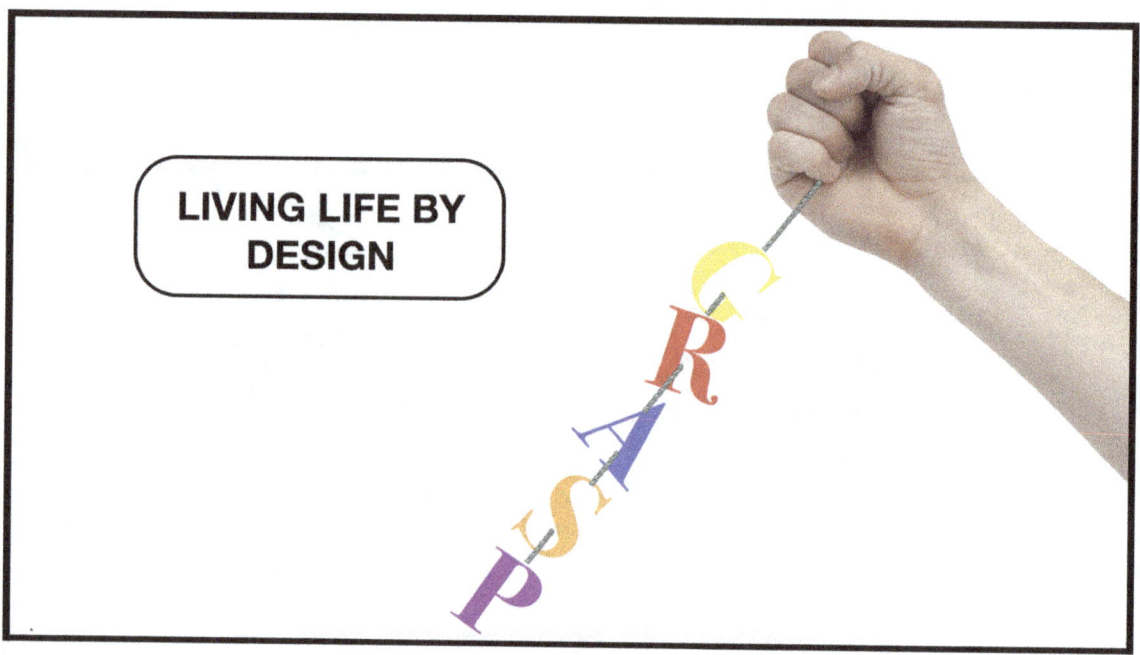

For a more in-depth description of GRASP, refer to pages 22 - 25 in our book, *How You Leave Them Feeling: Your Foundation for Inspiring Relationships.*

Use the GRASP - The Connection Worksheet on the following pages to create your Getting Ready Attitude Signature and Passion plan for your life.

# GRASP – The Connection Worksheet

GETTING READY: What are you getting ready for? (Promotion, a new relationship, retirement, an event, etc.)

_____

_____

_____

_____

_____

_____

ATTITUDE: What is your current attitude?

_____

_____

_____

_____

_____

_____

SIGNATURE: What top three personality traits represent your unique signature?

_____

_____

_____

_____

_____

**PASSION: Write down the top three areas of your life that bring you the most passion.**

_____

_____

_____

_____

_____

_____

_____

**Let's put it all together, starting with your attitude and moving to your signature while exercising what ignites your passion for building a great life.**

_____

_____

_____

_____

_____

_____

_____

# NOTES

# NOTES

## CHAPTER 2

# Trusting Your Gut Instincts

I have often used my intuition to make important life decisions. I can't recall a time when I trusted and acted upon my intuition and made the wrong choice. I can, however, recall countless times when I *ignored* my intuition and made the wrong choice.

The moral of this story is to learn to trust and act on the brain-gut connection, otherwise known as the power of intuition.

**Please respond to the questions provided below.**

1. **Do you recall a specific instance when you trusted your intuition and how it served you? Share the details.**

_____

_____

_____

_____

_____

_____

_____

_____

2. Think of a time when you didn't listen to your intuition. What was the outcome? What were the consequences?

_____

_____

_____

_____

_____

_____

_____

_____

3. Have you ever noticed a feeling of tightness in your stomach or chest when something undesirable is about to happen?

_____

_____

_____

_____

_____

_____

_____

_____

4. When evaluating important life decisions, how will you incorporate your gut feelings and intuition along with your thoughts and what's in your heart? We call this using your HHG (Head, Heart, and Gut).

_____

_____

_____

_____

_____

_____

_____

_____

_____

# NOTES

## CHAPTER 3

# Building Relationship Equity

Relationship equity is similar to the equity a homeowner builds up when they make upgrades and investments in their home. Over time, you add value to your home. You may build an outdoor patio in your backyard. You may consider adding a three-car garage or an indoor gym.

Each improvement you make adds to your home's equity and market value, just as quality investments made in your associations with others raise the significance of the relationship while increasing value on all sides.

The following exercise will help you bring relationship equity to your personal and professional connections. **Please respond to the questions provided below.**

1. **Who are your top 3 relationships?**

_____

_____

_____

_____

_____

_____

_____

2. **How can you add equity to these key relationships today?**

_____

_____

_____

_____

_____

_____

_____

_____

3. **Can you think of a friendship where you share a synergy and a flow?**
   **Yes_____ No_____**

If you answered yes, you have likely built outstanding relationship equity within that friendship.

If you can't think of a friendship like that, then it's time for you to start building relationship equity in your most important connections.

Below, we'll guide you through initiating relationship equity with our ICE concept.

### ICE – 3 Principles of Creating Relationship Equity

**I – Investing in Self and Others**
**C – Care About Self and Others**
**E – Extreme Self-Care**

Depending on your personality and life circumstances, investing in yourself may be near the end of your list, or you may not even place yourself on the list! **Please respond to the following questions.**

1. **What are your top 3 life priorities?**

_____

_____

_____

When we ask this question, 99 percent of the time, people never include themselves in their list of top priorities.

Are you part of that 99 percent? Yes_____ No _____

If you answered no to this question, congratulations. You are among the rare one percent of people who healthily prioritize themselves.

If you answered yes, consider our ICE principle.

**Please respond to the questions below.**

**I – Investing in Self and Others**

1. **What would it take to make your life a top-level priority?**

_____

_____

_____

_____

_____

_____

_____

Here's a universal truth: you likely won't get what you don't ask for! You've got to be willing to ask for what you want and need, consistently. Building relationship equity for yourself is as important as building it with others. Fill your cup first!

*"If momma ain't happy, ain't nobody happy." - unknown*

2. **What are your top three life priorities?**

_____

_____

_____

_____

_____

_____

_____

_____

3. **List three ways to start your day by paying yourself first. These are non-negotiable and life-changing once implemented.**

_____

_____

_____

_____

_____

_____

_____

_____

_____

You can borrow our 2-4 self-time concept. This means we spend two to four hours on ourselves every day.

## C – Care About Self and Others

Choosing to care about self and others is a magical connection to our How You Leave Them Feeling concept. It's all about considering how your actions may impact yourself and those around you. This simple concept encourages you to be mindful of your actions and their effects, helping you build the best possible relationship equity.

The caring portion of our **ICE** principle is much like the law of parsimony or the simplicity principle, called Ockham's Razor. William Ockham is credited with founding the law of parsimony, which states that the simplest solution is preferred over more complex ones.

4. **Can you think of a time when you over-thought a situation and made it more complicated than necessary? Explain it below.**

_____

_____

_____

_____

_____

5. **How could you have simplified the above scenario? Explain it below.**

_____

_____

_____

_____

_____

## E – Extreme Self-Care

As you continue to enrich your life through healthy relationship-building, we invite you to take extreme care of yourself. Keep it simple and mirror the law of parsimony: You must care about yourself and others to live a joyful and enriched life!

If you don't choose self-care, it may be easy for you to fall into unhealthy patterns such as being insecure, unaware, self-conscious, or anxious. When you add any or all of the self-care recommendations below to your daily routine, you will experience a more vibrant energy within yourself.

# Practicing Self-Care Involves the Following:

1. Developing emotional intelligence (EI). EI equips you with the power to understand and manage your emotions positively, amplifies your ability to communicate effectively with others, and defuses conflict. The path to EI is not just about personal growth; it's about fostering a more harmonious and empathetic world around you.

2. Prioritizing self-compassion in your self-care journey is a pivotal step. It's about recognizing your inherent worth, embracing your imperfections, and treating yourself with the same kindness and understanding you extend to a loved one. Remember, you are worthy of your compassion.

3. Practicing good sleeping habits and taking breaks throughout your day.

4. Being mindful of healthy eating choices.

5. Cutting out negative self-talk by discovering your best assets and living from what you do have, not from what you don't have.

6. Reserving self-time. Block time on your calendar just for yourself, and use this time to do what you want to do to serve yourself.

7. Integrating meditation into your daily routine can be a game-changer, even if you allocate just fifteen to thirty minutes daily. It's a sacred time to disconnect from the outside world, find inner peace, and recharge your mental and emotional batteries. The rejuvenating effects of meditation are truly life-altering. Listen to Lisa's meditation by scanning the QR Code on page 90.

8. Nurturing your basic physical needs by walking, biking, or other daily exercises to maintain good physical health.

9. Considering your psychological development. To grow your mental state, participate in activities such as movies, plays, books, and special events.

10. Cultivating resilience. Continue discovering ways to become more resilient by not allowing life difficulties to bring you to your knees.

You are ready to start adding value to your key relationships and to yourself.

**Please respond to the questions below.**

1. **What is the very best way you will start adding value to your key relationships?**

_____

_____

_____

_____

_____

_____

_____

2. **List the ways you will start adding value for yourself.**

_____

_____

_____

_____

_____

_____

_____

*"People don't care how much you know until they know how much you care." —President Theodore Roosevelt*

# NOTES

# NOTES

## CHAPTER 4

# The Umuntu Factor

In 2014, we traveled to South Africa with a group of 18 people, many of whom soon became our close friends. The most powerful jewel that came from our South African journey is expressed in three inspiring words: "Umuntu, ngumuntu, ngabantu." Umuntu is translated to mean, "I am because you are." *The entire Zulu tribe phrase, "Umuntu, ngumuntu, ngabantu" means that a person is a person through other people.*

The truth is that when you allow the connection from one soul to another, you open the opportunity for enrichment and positive energy to fuel you. We have heard it said with a keen sense of awareness, *"You are one handshake away from an entirely different lifestyle."* This quote says it all.

The handshakes, acquaintances, colleagues, bosses, friends, and intimate relationships we encounter offer the opportunity to dramatically impact our lives! However, the opportunity for this handshake theory to impact your life is squashed if you refuse to live into the perspective that we are all designed to be relational beings.

Society's influence on the individual helps ensure we have the same beliefs and values as those around us. This is a great catalyst for building social harmony. Understanding the impact of how we are hardwired to be social animals helps us embrace the full power of the Umuntu factor.

Umuntu has its roots in humanist African philosophy, where the idea of community is one of the building blocks of society. Umuntu is that nebulous concept of common humanity, oneness: humanity, you, and me. We have embraced this inspiring concept and often pair it up with building unity with our inspirational audiences from around the world, simply saying, *"Together we are better."* Ensuring a connection with those who matter involves creating multiple options.

### "Umuntu ngumuntu ngabantu.' Umuntu is translated to mean, 'I am, because you are." —Zulu tribe

**Write down a few meaningful ways to stay connected with the people that matter to you.**

_____

_____

_____

_____

_____

**List the people you have lost touch with and with whom you need to rekindle the relationship.**

_____

_____

_____

_____

_____

*"Be mindful that we are all one handshake away from living an entirely different life." - Anthony Ciccone*

# NOTES

# NOTES

## CHAPTER 5

# The Relationship Excellence Suite: Portfolio

To ensure that we include measurable structure in our quest for Relationship Excellence, we designed the Relationship Excellence Suite to house the key components that offer a roadmap to sustainable and measurable success.

We will cover the various Relationship Excellence Suite components over the next few chapters consisting of the following:

1. 5-Star What Matters Most Assessment
2. House Rules
3. Color Code Personality Assessment
4. The Five Love Languages
5. Relationship Games

As we delve into the five key sections of the Relationship Excellence Suite, we'll use the **5-Star What Matters Most Assessment you completed in Chapter One.**

This assessment is not just a tool; it's a catalyst for personal growth. It's the basis for understanding yourself, aligning your behaviors, and relating to others clearly and meaningfully, inspiring you to become the best version of yourself.

Refer to Chapter One, Living Life by Design, to review your 5-Star What Matters Most Assessment.

Besides following my gut instincts, as mentioned in Chapter Two, Hyrum Smith's book *What Matters Most* was the key to discovering what I truly wanted. To ensure you're asking yourself the right questions and maintaining personal alignment with what you want, **please respond to the questions below.**

1.  **What do you want for and from your life? (You answered this in Chapter One, however, your answer may have shifted as you've completed the exercises in this workbook.)**

_____

_____

_____

_____

When you consistently act in contrast to your values, you remain out of alignment and will experience a feeling of "something wrong" in your gut. Over time, this becomes your normal behavior, and you can lose track of how out of balance you are. An example is when a man places honesty as a high value but consistently cheats on his wife. He is out of alignment because having intimate affairs outside of his marriage is dishonest.

2.  **Have you ever experienced being out of alignment? How did that feel?**

_____

_____

_____

_____

When your values and roles are in a positive, complete alignment with your actions, this is the foundation for building and living a life by design!

If you find yourself out of alignment with your highest roles and values, take the time to determine exactly what action steps you must take to bring yourself back into alignment.

3.  **How can you start bringing yourself back into alignment? (Example: Commit to being honest about the areas of your life where you are failing and look at the key components of what may be causing that failure. Check your values to determine if your actions and roles are consistent with your value system.**

**Provide Examples of How You Must Return to Alignment Below:**

_____

_____

_____

_____

_____

_____

_____

*"Communication is the solvent of all problems and is the foundation for personal development." – Peter Shepherd*

After reviewing your What Matters Most Thoughtwork from Chapter One, **please transfer your top five most important roles and values into the Top 5 Most Important What Matters Most Roles & Values Assessment below:**

## Top 5 Most Important
## What Matters Most Roles & Values Assessment

_____    _____

_____    _____

_____    _____

_____    _____

If you find yourself out of alignment between your highest roles and values, take the time to determine exactly what action steps you must take to bring yourself back into alignment. It would be best to consult with a trusted advisor or accountability partner to ensure you are being honest with yourself.

# NOTES

# NOTES

## CHAPTER 6

# The Relationship Excellence Suite: Color Code Personality Assessment

Taylor Hartman, PhD, invented the Color Code Personality Assessment. The Color Code divides personalities into four colors based on the idea that everyone possesses one of four Driving Core Motives (DCM): what you do and why you do it. Their DCM represents clear distinctions of their dominant disposition, depicting a person's traits and how those traits correspond with their overall personality.

The Color Code focuses on helping you know your character at the innate level - the unique character you were born with. This accurate knowledge enables you to gain more profound and valuable insights into what makes you and those around you tick.

We call this the process of learning to speak the language of others. When others feel like you understand them and can relate to them in the way they most desire, your communication is raised to the highest level. It establishes a good rhythm or flow while communicating with others.

Speaking the language of others offers you the tools to communicate in a way they will quickly understand. This quick understanding happens because you communicate based on their Driving Core Motives. We call this 'meeting them where they're at' during communication.

If you haven't already done so, please take the Color Code Personality Assessment to understand yourself at an innate level and learn to communicate with others in the way they prefer.

**Scan the QR code below to take the Color Code Assessment.**

Following the descriptions, below find a summary of the four colors

# BLUES (DCM is Intimacy)

The following describes what it means to be motivated by intimacy as a Blue.

Being motivated by intimacy means that Blues like to connect with others on a deep and meaningful level. Ask any Blue how they feel about people who are fake/superficial, and you will get quite a strong reaction.

Blues want nothing to do with fake people because intimacy for a Blue is about truth, legitimacy, integrity, loyalty, and sincerity. Most Blues will tell you that they can count the number of their true friends on one hand because those are the people with whom they feel that real, intimate connection.

Blues need to be understood and appreciated. Everything they do is quality-based. They are loyal friends, employers, and employees. Whatever or whomever they commit to is their sole (and soul) focus. They love to serve and give of themselves freely to nurture others' lives.

Blues have distinct preferences and the most controlling personality. Their code of ethics is remarkably strong, and they expect others to live honest, committed lives as well. They enjoy sharing meaningful moments in conversation and paying close attention to special life events like birthdays and anniversaries.

Blues are dependable, thoughtful, and analytical, but can also be self-righteous, worry-prone, and moody. When you deal with Blues, be sincere and genuinely try to understand and appreciate them.

*"I'm not a perfectionist; you just aren't meeting my expectations."*

# WHITES (DCM is Peace)

The following describes what it means to be motivated by peace as a White.

While most Whites are not typically big fans of conflict, their definition of peace runs deeper than simply the absence of conflict. To a White, peace is all about inner harmony and balance.

Whites, in their quest for equilibrium, are averse to having it disrupted. This is why they often steer conversations away from topics that might unsettle them, preferring to keep the peace within.

They seek independence and require kindness. They resist confrontation at all costs. To them, feeling good is more important than being good. They are typically quiet by nature and process deeply and objectively with great clarity.

Of all the colors, Whites are the best listeners. They respect direct people but recoil from perceived hostility or verbal battles. Whites need their alone time and refuse to be controlled by others. They want to do things their way and in their own time. They ask little of others and resent others demanding much of them.

Whites are much stronger than people think; they are not often seen for their strength because they don't readily reveal their feelings. They are even-tempered, diplomatic, and the voice of reason, but they can also be indecisive, unexpressive, and silently stubborn. When you deal with Whites, be kind, accept and support their individuality, and look for nonverbal clues to understand their feelings.

*"Beauty begins the moment you decide to be yourself."*

# REDS (DCM is Power)

The following describes what it means to be motivated by power as a Red.

Sometimes, people think about power in terms of control. While it's true that Reds like to be in control of their circumstances and are attracted to leadership opportunities, that's not a complete picture of what power means to Reds. To Reds, power generally means the ability to move from point A to point B - and to do it directly and efficiently as possible.

The Spanish and Portuguese translations for the word "power" as a verb are "poder," which means "to be able to do." That is a fitting description of what power means to a Red. They want to be productive and efficient.

They seek productivity and need to look good to others. Simply stated, the Reds want their way. They like to be in the driver's seat and willingly pay the price to be in a leadership role.

Reds value whatever gets them ahead, whether in their careers, school endeavors, or personal life. What Reds value, they get done. They are often workaholics. They will, however, resist doing anything that doesn't interest them.

Reds like to be right. They value approval from others for their intelligence and practical approach to life and want to be respected. Reds are confident, proactive, and visionary, but they can also be arrogant, selfish, and insensitive. When you deal with Reds, be precise, factual, and direct, and show no fear.

*"Oh, my email sounds harsh. Let me add a smiley face."*

# YELLOWS (DCM is Fun)

The following describes what it means to be motivated by fun as a Yellow. The fun does not simply mean that Yellows seek endless frivolity and never take things seriously.

People incorrectly assume that Yellows don't like structure when, in fact, they crave it. It only looks like they resist it because most Yellows don't know how to create structure independently. Fun to a Yellow means "living in the moment."

It means that they enjoy the process of what they are doing far more than the result. That's why Yellows are generally so engaged and "present" when you are with them. Carpe diem, or "seize the day," is a Yellow way of life.

Yellows are inviting and embrace life as a party that they're hosting. They love playful interaction and can be extremely sociable. They are highly persuasive and seek instant gratification. Yellows need to be adored and praised. While Yellows are carefree, they are sensitive and highly alert to others' agendas to control them. Yellows typically carry a good heart.

Yellows need to look good socially, and friendships are a high priority in their lives. They are happy, articulate, engaging with others, and crave adventure. Easily distracted, they can only sit still for a short time. They embrace each day in the present tense and choose to be around people who enjoy a curious nature like themselves.

Yellows are charismatic, spontaneous, and positive but can also be irresponsible, obnoxious, and forgetful. When dealing with Yellows, take a positive, upbeat approach and promote light-hearted, creative, and fun interactions.

*"I don't mean to interrupt. I just like what I have to say better."*

55

See the chart below for a quick reference of the four colors.

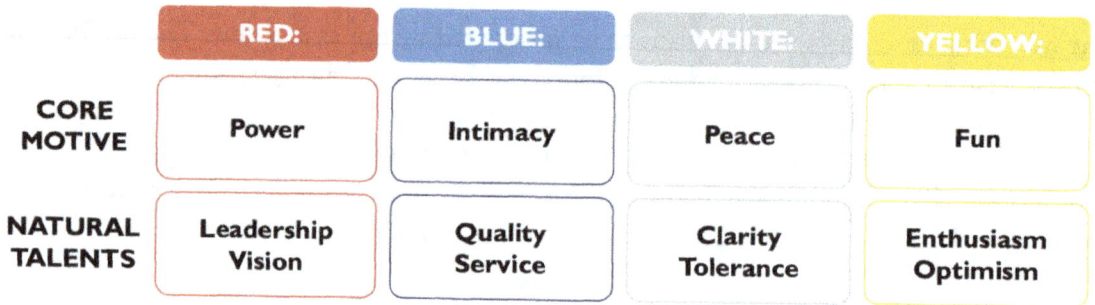

|  | RED: | BLUE: | WHITE: | YELLOW: |
|---|---|---|---|---|
| CORE MOTIVE | Power | Intimacy | Peace | Fun |
| NATURAL TALENTS | Leadership Vision | Quality Service | Clarity Tolerance | Enthusiasm Optimism |

**Now that you've identified your colors, what do you agree or disagree with? Please note your response below:**

_____

_____

_____

_____

You will learn to communicate very effectively with a broad range of personalities by removing limitations from your character and using the strengths from your four colors

Choose two limitations you want to eliminate from your communication with others and write them below:

_____

_____

Choose two strengths you want to ensure remain present in your communication with others and write them below:

_____

_____

When you're prepared to delve deeper, find an accountability partner at home and another at work. Let them serve as your reliable witnesses, keeping you on track as you work toward becoming a healthier, more character-driven person according to Color Code standards.

The best way to improve your character is to become healthy and charactered. You must reduce all of your limitations, use your native strengths, and borrow new strengths that are not native to you.

*"Compliment people. Magnify their strengths, not their weaknesses." – anonymous*

57

## CHAPTER 7

# The Relationship Excellence Suite: House Rules, Love Languages, and Games

House Rules, Love Languages, and Games are designed to develop and promote synergy, engagement, and joy in essential, intimate relationships. These components can assist individuals, couples, business partners, and friends improve their day-to-day interactions and increase positivity and connection.

## House Rules

Early in our relationship, we talked about the many couples we've met who lacked a rhythm to live together harmoniously. Each of their wants and needs would drive the other crazy, and the other partner largely ignored those wants and needs.

As we studied this phenomenon and reflected on our past relationships, we quickly realized that neither of us had ever experienced the elusive harmony. The truth is that we made the same mistakes that countless others have made. We never established agreements regarding our specific wants and needs in our relationships.

This was a defining moment, and we decided to right this wrong handed down through the ages, generation after generation. We vowed to identify and share a minimum of one and a maximum of three of our strongest desires to create our own harmonious living space.

We created and agreed upon how this revolutionary way of living would work. Taking the time to develop meaningful and connected agreements about how we wanted to live felt awesome!

We chose to call these agreements House Rules. If you are not fond of subscribing to "rules," you may consider calling them House Agreements.

The terminology of House Agreements works very well because it establishes: an understanding and agreement of what is best for you and your partner.

## House Rules Bylaws

1.  Each partner's chosen House Rule is non-negotiable and respected precisely as designed.

2.  Each partner must submit at least one and no more than three House Rules that they request to be respected.

3.  You must know and respect each other's House Rules.

4.  Discuss your House Rules every 90 days, allowing both partners to be heard and included in the decision-making process. This will ensure we honor and respect each other's House Rules.

5.  You can swap out one or more of your House Rules every 90 days as desired.

One of Lisa's house rules is that she requires the first hour of each new day to wake up to the world privately. She uses this time for meditation, tub time, self-discovery, and setting her intentions for the day.

One of Jesse's House Rules is SWITCH. The purpose of SWITCH is to request that any time Lisa sees or feels that he may be doing something or not doing something that is hurting their relationship or business in any manner, she must bring that to his attention.

If the uninformed partner doesn't know what they need to **SWITCH,** they ask the informed partner. After the informed partner explains what to **SWITCH,** the uninformed partner confirms by saying **"SWITCH."**

For a deeper breakdown of House Rules, see page 87 in our book *How You Leave Them Feeling: Your Foundation for Inspiring Relationships.*

*"Authenticity is the choice to show up and be real. The choice to be honest. The choice to let our true selves be seen." – Brene Brown*

Describe your House Rules and how implementing them can improve the quality of the relationship with your significant other, children, or other family members you live with. Use the space below to highlight your House Rules.

# HOUSE RULES

# NOTES

# NOTES

## The 5 Love Languages

You may be familiar with *"The Golden Rule,"* which says you should " treat others how you like to be treated." It would be simple and easy if everyone else were just like you.

Since we are all unique, we suggest you consider learning and adopting *"The Platinum Rule."* The Platinum Rule recommends treating others how they want to be treated. How will you know? Typically, they will tell you! If you want to enjoy great intimate relationships, learn how your significant other would like to be treated.

One of the simplest relationship systems, tools, and processes to do this is The 5 Love Languages, a concept developed by Gary Chapman, PhD, author, speaker, and counselor. Dr. Chapman explains that everyone expresses and receives love differently, and by identifying and adhering to these differences, you can communicate your love more effectively. The 5 Love Languages are:

1. **Acts of service**
2. **Receiving gifts**
3. **Quality time**
4. **Words of affirmation**
5. **Physical touch**

This concept is helpful for all types of relationships, including romantic relationships, family and friends, and even coworkers. By identifying and using your partner's love language, you can improve the quality of your relationship and show them how much you care. We recommend you take The 5 Love Languages quiz. It's free and will take you less than five minutes. **Scan the QR code below to take the quiz.**

63

Please list your 5 Love Languages below, and if you have a partner, list their 5 Love Languages as well.

## The 5 Love Languages

**My 5 Love Languages**

**My Partner's 5 Love Languages (optional)**

_____          _____

_____          _____

_____          _____

_____          _____

_____          _____

_____          _____

_____          _____

Knowing someone's Love Language is not enough. Our current society is overloaded with information and crazy, busy schedules. When it comes to knowing exactly how to relate to your significant other, business partner, or friend and express love in the fashion of their choosing, your best intentions will likely fall by the wayside. There are certain traps we must avoid.

One trap that can confuse the knowledge of our partner's love language is how comfortable we get in our relationships. ***Relationship Comfort*** occurs when we get lax in a close or intimate relationship (like we may do with our husbands, wives, parents, girlfriends, boyfriends, best friends, coworkers, bosses, sisters, brothers, etc.) and take them and their feelings for granted.

We often overlook the continuous effort required in all relationships, particularly our closest ones. Remembering the importance of kindness and care is crucial, as they are the cornerstone of healthy relationships.

Relationship Comfort occurs when we stop hearing or faithfully listening to the other person or when we act like they will always be there. Getting too comfortable in a relationship can be like a screen that blocks a beautiful view across the landscape of life.

**Do you recognize any of the following breakdowns or traps happening in your most important relationships:**

- **Communication:** Complacency can lead to less open and meaningful communication. Partners may assume they know what the other is thinking or feeling, which can result in misunderstandings and unresolved issues.

- **Emotional Connection:** If you become too comfortable, the emotional bond between partners can weaken. You may stop putting in the effort to connect on a deeper level, leading to feelings of distance or detachment.

- **Intimacy:** Physical and emotional intimacy might decline as partners stop trying to keep the relationship exciting and fulfilling. This can lead to a lack of passion and decreased physical touch or affection.

- **Quality Time:** Routine and complacency can cause partners to spend less quality time together. This might mean fewer date nights, shared activities, or simple moments of togetherness vital for maintaining a strong bond.

- **Respect and Appreciation:** Over-familiarity can lead to a decrease in respect and appreciation for one another. Partners might take each other for granted or overlook the small gestures that once made the relationship special.

- **Growth and Change:** A comfortable marriage can hinder personal growth and change. If partners don't encourage each other to pursue new experiences or interests, the relationship might stagnate, leading to boredom, discontent, and divorce.

When these areas begin to break down, addressing them early is essential. Revitalizing communication, re-establishing emotional connections, and making an effort to prioritize the relationship can help reignite the spark and prevent further deterioration and resentment.

65

**Take a few minutes and write down which of the breakdowns listed on the previous page affect your most important relationships.**

_____

_____

_____

_____

_____

_____

_____

**What actions will you implement to make a difference in your lives right now?**

_____

_____

_____

_____

_____

_____

_____

Your best avenue to the winner's circle of life is to *raise your Relationship Comfort awareness.* Remember to embrace and add value to your most important relationships. Remain mindful in appreciating and nurturing your valued connections. Also, be aware of human nature related to forgetting or disrespecting longer-term relationships.

Do your best not to fall into a happenstance attitude of the same old and familiar routines. This *reduced awareness is a relationship killer!*

Raising your awareness includes simple gestures of appreciation like saying *"thank you"* and *"please."* Always remember that it is human nature to become complacent in long-term relationships. We get bored of the same old familiar relationships.

*Understanding The 5 Love Languages* and identifying the language of your friends and partners equips us with additional tools to prevent us from falling into the negative side of Relationship Comfort, empowering us to *take control of our most important relationships.*

*"I've been doing marriage counseling for the last 15 years, and I realized that what makes one person feel loved, doesn't make the other person feel loved." – Gary Chapman*

# NOTES

## Relationship Game #1

Our Relationship Excellence Suite consists of two games. ***The first one is Dialogue.*** This game was designed for couples who want to continue learning more about one another in conversations that likely wouldn't have happened without it.

Start the game by flipping a coin to determine who goes first. The winner of the coin toss chooses a favorite song from their past, and the partner listening to the music has to attempt to guess the artist and name of the song. The partner that guesses correctly receives 2.5 points for each correct answer.

The partner who chose the song now tells a compelling story about what was going on in their life during the period. The partner listening to the song rates the quality of the story from one to five, with five representing a great story. Once the other partner has shared and rated the story, you trade sides, and your partner switches to the person choosing the song.

As you take turns and share your stories, you're not just playing a game but engaging in a mutual learning experience. When the game is over, tally up the points to determine the winner, but remember, the real value is in the new insights you've gained about each other.

We've personally experienced the transformative power of this game with other couples. It's a catalyst for deeper connections and leaves everyone feeling positive and enriched. As you share infectious energy and connect with others, you won't want to let go of these newfound bonds.

*"It is not a lack of love, but a lack of friendship that makes unhappy marriages." – Friedrich Nitzsche*

# Relationship Game #2

*"Wow - What I Like About You"* is not just a game; it's a relationship booster. It's a fun way to learn each other's likes and how best to incorporate them into your relationship. Once you've experienced the thrill of this game, it will inspire you to continue discovering new details about your partner, fostering a deeper connection!

Set aside thirty minutes to recall and share the awesome actions and gestures you received from one another. This game also uses a scoring system of one to five. Five is the highest wow factor, and one is a vote of appreciation.

**Following are a few examples of conversation starters and questions you can use to learn what one another likes**

- What is your favorite color?
- What is your favorite food?
- Describe your next bucket list vacation in detail.
- When will you schedule this dream vacation?
- How do you like me to show you love and attention?
- How can I support you?
- What can I do around the house to help you?
- I love to be surprised by......
- I love it when you tell me I look beautiful.
- I appreciate it when you turn the bed down and turn on the heated blanket so my cold feet get warm and I can fall asleep faster.
- If you could wave a magic wand, what would you wish for and why?
- I appreciate encouraging words to help me get through trying times.

You can protect your relationship further by scheduling and planning a date night each week. Make all the arrangements, i.e., a babysitter for the children, a dinner or show reservation, a picnic in the park, etc.

Incorporating these ideas into your relationship can create a deeper sense of love and affection, fostering a strong and lasting connection.

# NOTES

# NOTES

# CHAPTER 8

# Friendship, Love, and Marriage: Those Special Bonds

There are countless ways to determine the meaning of friendship, love, and marriage. If you ask one hundred people for their definitions, those words would likely mean something different to everyone.

The top three universal fundamentals in close relationships are transparency, vulnerability, and truth. We have observed and adopted these universal principles and have seen their impact in building and maintaining long-lasting friendships, love, and marriages.

**What do transparency, vulnerability, and truth mean to you in your closest relationships?**

_____

_____

_____

_____

_____

_____

_____

_____

_____

_____

_____

_____

_____

How will you incorporate these principles into your interactions with others?

_____

_____

_____

_____

_____

_____

_____

_____

_____

Given that everyone has a unique understanding of friendship, love, and marriage, how do you and your spouse/partner align your views to ensure a solid and meaningful relationship?

_____

_____

_____

_____

_____

_____

_____

_____

_____

**How will practicing the universal principles of transparency, vulnerability, and truth impact your important relationships?**

_____

_____

_____

_____

_____

_____

If you are looking to create an amazing life with your chosen partner, you must be focused and adopt a theme of *Constant and Never-Ending Evolution* to grow your power of presence. We call this living in the spirit of *CANEE*.

Consider the value you will bring to your important relationships by offering **transparency, vulnerability, and truth**.

## Friendship, Love, and Marriage
## Those Special Bonds Exercise

1. **Think about your definitions of friendship, love, and marriage. Do they match those of your friends and loved ones? What do you need to do to close any gaps between the two? Write your answers below.**

_____

_____

_____

_____

_____

_____

2. Are you seeking to please everyone while drowning in overserving? Are you covering your real feelings about this challenge with a Superman or Superwoman cape? If your answer to these questions is yes, write your answers below and brainstorm how you can eliminate this behavior, remove your cape, and be truthful and authentic with yourself and others:

_____

_____

_____

_____

_____

_____

_____

# NOTES

## CHAPTER 9

# Building Unbreakable Relationships

The best path to fostering unbreakable relationships starts and ends with paying close attention to the concept of *How You Leave Them Feeling.* As you begin practicing leaving situations better than you found them and leaving others wanting more of your presence, you will exhibit character traits and behaviors that help you master this concept.

The significance of building unbreakable relationships starts with the desire to make robust and sustainable connections within all of your relationships.

**What is the value of building unbreakable relationships?**

_____

_____

_____

_____

_____

_____

To find the best formula for success in building unbreakable relationships, you must be willing to express your real feelings.

**What is your predominant emotion(s) when you think of your significant other, business partner, family members, and friends? See examples of emotions below.**

_____

_____

_____

_____

_____

_____

_____

**Examples of emotions:**

1. Joy
2. Sadness
3. Anger
4. Fear
5. Disgust
6. Surprise
7. Love
8. Hate
9. Trust
10. Anticipation
11. Contempt
12. Shame
13. Guilt
14. Pride
15. Compassion
16. Envy

17. Jealousy
18. Relief
19. Nostalgia
20. Frustration
21. Excitement
22. Amusement
23. Awe
24. Boredom
25. Gratitude
26. Embarrassment
27. Determination
28. Pity
29. Regret
30. Hopelessness

Developing your Emotional Intelligence (EI) is critical to building and maintaining long-term relationships. In chapter three we touched upon the value of developing your EI while practicing self-care. Having advanced EI will help develop unbreakable relationships.

Now is the ideal time to focus on enhancing your emotional intelligence (EI) skills. By doing so, you can improve your ability to understand and manage your emotions, as well as those of others. This can lead to more positive interactions, better communication, and stronger connections in both your personal and professional life.

1. **Why is developing emotional intelligence (EI) crucial for building and sustaining your important relationships?**

_____

_____

_____

_____

_____

_____

2. **How can harnessing Emotional Intelligence (EI) improve your communication skills and help you build stronger, more meaningful relationships with others?**

_____

_____

_____

_____

_____

_____

**List the ways you will start practicing developing your emotional intelligence ( EI) today.**

_____

_____

_____

_____

_____

_____

_____

_____

_____

_____

_____

By harnessing the power of *Emotional Intelligence* (EI), you can enhance your communication skills and build better relationships. The better you are at managing your own emotions, the better equipped you are to empathize and connect with others.

When the people you interact with feel you understand, care about, and value them, the bond you create has the potential to become unbreakable.

As you pursue the building or rebuilding of your relationships, consider incorporating these *seven unbreakable principles* into all your interactions with others:

**Kindness**
**Empathy**
**Care**
**Consistency**
**Awareness**
**Intuition**
**Love**

**These seven components lead to unbreakable relationships:**

**Kindness**

Consistently delivering kindness to others not only offers the strong possibility of having kindness returned to you, but it also leaves you feeling good about bringing kind gestures to those who may be battling challenging matters. Your kindness is a welcomed gift to help lighten the load.

**Empathy**

When others receive empathy from you, it lets them know you have compassion for their particular circumstances. It offers a safe place for them to tell the truth about matters of concern.

**Care**

Care is the genuine concern and attention given to the well-being, comfort, and needs of someone or something. It involves empathy, compassion, and a willingness to act to ensure the physical, emotional, and psychological health of others.

**Consistency**

Consistency is vital in building trust and strong relationships with others. When you consistently prioritize what matters most to them and make positive contributions, it makes them feel confident in relying on you.

**Awareness**

Awareness is key to developing empathy and understanding the needs and concerns of others. Unlike self-centeredness, awareness allows us to focus on the needs of those around us and offer support. While many people are primarily concerned with meeting their own needs, awareness allows us to focus on the needs of others, which is a sharp contrast to self-centeredness.

**Intuition**

When you can tap into the wants and needs of others through a feeling or instinct, that is using your intuition. Other people are generally appreciative of receiving your outreach.

**Love**

We truly believe that sharing love with others is a universal concept. Others can feel love even when they aren't speaking the same language or come from a different origin. Sharing love with others reaches people at the heart and feeling level. Receiving an act of love leaves us feeling valued.

**Below, list one or more of these seven core principles that need to be injected into your important relationships and note why this will raise the quality of those relationships.**

_____

_____

_____

_____

_____

_____

_____

_____

_____

_____

_____

_____

## Building Unbreakable Relationships Exercise

1. On the following **NOTES page**, list all of your significant relationships and decide which ones are worth taking to the "unbreakable" level.

2. Review your significant relationship list and ensure the seven unbreakable relationship principles are enrolled. Make sure you take the proactive steps of applying these seven unbreakable principles now.

3. Read about emotional intelligence and see whether your behavior and attitudes are conducive to creating good relationship energy and equity in your life.

*"It's good to be kind to everyone you meet... because everybody is battling something." —Unknown*

# NOTES

# NOTES

## CHAPTER 10

# Turning a Crisis into Abundance

Have you ever found yourself at a crossroads when handling a challenging situation?

Let's call these crossroads "experiences of managing catastrophic events." They can cause stress levels to rise. They often involve managing real-life difficulties and losses such as the death of friends or family members, the death of a child, fear of the unknown, unemployment, loneliness, depression, a health challenge, managing blended families, or divorce.

This chapter will offer you the opportunity to turn crisis into abundance!

According to the American Psychological Association, chronic stress is linked to the six leading causes of death: heart disease, cancer, lung ailments, accidents, cirrhosis of the liver, and suicide. Why would you allow something as invasive and debilitating as stress to put you at a higher risk for premature death?

**List three things that continually leave you feeling stressed.**

_____

_____

_____

_____

_____

_____

_____

_____

## What will you do to reduce and eliminate these stresses?

Review our AAA Life Strategy Concept on page 117 in our book, *How You Leave Them Feeling: Your Foundation for Inspiring Relationships,* for ideas on eliminating stress.

_____

_____

_____

_____

_____

_____

**Describe below a couple of crisis matters you have either dealt with in the past, or you are dealing with right now. Following your review, list what key steps you can take to resolve the crisis.**

_____

_____

_____

_____

_____

_____

_____

_____

_____

_____

_____

We have found great value in using meditation to help us achieve a much better mental attitude after navigating stress or crisis. Please find the benefits of meditation on the following pages, along with a QR code to scan and listen to a brief meditation piece titled "Meditation for Renewal and Well-Being," designed especially for you.

Meditation has numerous benefits across physical, mental, and spiritual dimensions. Here's a clear explanation of why meditation is good for your health, body, mind, and soul:

## Physical Benefits:

1. **Reduces Stress**: Meditation activates the body's relaxation response, reducing the production of stress hormones like cortisol and helping to lower overall stress levels.

2. **Improves Sleep**: Regular meditation can enhance sleep quality by promoting relaxation and reducing insomnia symptoms.

3. **Boosts Immune System**: Meditation improves immune function through its stress-reducing effects.

4. **Lowers Blood Pressure**: Meditation techniques such as mindfulness and deep breathing can help lower blood pressure by promoting relaxation and reducing strain on the heart.

5. **Pain Management**: Meditation can alleviate chronic pain by enhancing pain tolerance and reducing pain perception.

## Mental Benefits:

1. **Enhances Focus and Concentration**: Meditation practices improve cognitive function, attention span, and the ability to concentrate on tasks.

2. **Reduces Anxiety and Depression**: Regular meditation can alleviate symptoms of anxiety and depression by promoting relaxation and emotional well-being.

3. **Promotes Emotional Health**: Meditation cultivates mindfulness, which helps individuals observe their thoughts and emotions without judgment, leading to greater emotional resilience and stability.

4. **Increases Self-Awareness**: Meditation encourages self-reflection and introspection, assisting individuals to gain insight into their behaviors, thoughts, and emotions.

5. **Improves Cognitive Function**: Meditation enhances memory, problem-solving, and decision-making abilities.

**Spiritual and Emotional Benefits:**

1. **Enhances Spiritual Growth**: For many, meditation is a spiritual practice that deepens their connection to their inner self, higher consciousness, or spiritual beliefs.

2. **Promotes Inner Peace**: Meditation cultivates a sense of inner peace and calmness, helping individuals navigate life's challenges with equanimity.

3. **Fosters Compassion and Empathy**: Loving-kindness meditation can enhance feelings of compassion towards oneself and others, promoting social connectedness and empathy.

4. **Increases Happiness and Well-being**: Regular meditation increases life satisfaction, happiness, and overall well-being.

**Overall Impact:**

Meditation's holistic benefits on health, body, mind, and soul are not just a matter of belief but a scientifically proven fact. Numerous studies have shown that by inducing a state of deep relaxation, promoting mindfulness, and facilitating self-awareness, meditation brings about profound improvements in physical health, mental clarity, emotional stability, and spiritual growth.

This integration of meditation into daily life can lead to a more balanced and fulfilling life, backed by the confidence of scientific evidence.

**Scan the QR code below to listen to a brief guided meditation piece written and narrated by Lisa Ferrell. Meditation for Renewal & Well-being**

**The following are guided meditations we've listened to and gained enormous value from over the last 17 years. For best results, we recommend using noise-canceling headphones while meditating.**

- **Dudley Evenson** - *Meditation Moments*

- **Lisa Ulshafer** - *Journey of Remembrance*

- **Joe Dispenza** - *Quantum Field*

- **Davidji** - *Flow of Love*

- **Solfeggio Frequency** meditation uses specific sound frequencies to promote healing, relaxation, and spiritual well-being. Each Solfeggio frequency resonates with particular physical, mental, and emotional states, and practitioners use these tones to balance and harmonize their energy.

  **Specific Frequencies: The Solfeggio scale consists of six main frequencies:**

  396 Hz - Liberating Guilt and Fear

  417 Hz - Undoing Situations and Facilitating Change

  528 Hz - Transformation and Miracles (DNA Repair)

  639 Hz - Connecting/Relationships

  741 Hz - Expression/Solutions

  852 Hz - Returning to Spiritual Order

- **Tibetan Bowls** played while you sleep helps to defrag your brain. The idea that Tibetan bowls played while you sleep can "defrag" your brain is more metaphorical than scientifically proven.

- **Metaphorical Defragging**: The term "defragging" is borrowed from computer terminology, where it refers to reorganizing data to improve efficiency. In the context of the brain, it suggests that the soothing sounds might help to clear mental clutter, promote mental clarity, and enhance cognitive function

- **Kelly Howell** - *The Universal Mind (Binaural Beats)*: An audio technology called binaural beats can help quiet the mind quickly and relieve stress by inducing the brainwave states experienced during meditation (Alpha, Beta, Theta, Delta).

## Lisa's Story of Her Corporate Work Stress:

Every year, Lisa would come down with bronchitis as the year-end approached. She was serving as an account executive selling television airtime, and the year-end expectations to meet quotas and goals brought on anxiety, fear, and loads of stress!

Management would revise budgets five and six times before coming to terms with one that would stick. Lisa worked 14 to 16 hours per day to hit her deadlines. This schedule would eventually cause chronic stress lasting weeks.

While enduring the exhaustion of working long hours, her January sales performance expectations and the holiday demands created unimaginable stress. Even Christmas and gift-giving activities stressed her out.

In October of 2005, moving into the New Year celebration was too much for her. Her chronic stress progressed into an illness that had her bedridden for weeks.

**Can you relate to this cyclical stress that can bring you to your knees like Lisa? Yes____No____**

**Share your story below about something that has repeatedly caused you stress:**

_____

_____

_____

_____

_____

_____

*"Your WHY is not about what you do, but about how you do it and the impact you have on others." – Simon Sinek*

## Jesse's Corporate Story That Transformed Everything:

After working for over 36 years with a degree in hotel administration from the University of Las Vegas, Jesse was fired from his executive casino marketing position. He couldn't believe that all of the unpaid overtime, industry experience, and superb colleague and client relationships just weren't enough. During the termination meeting, he said two words with strong conviction, "Never again."

Never again would he allow one man, one woman, or a committee decide his financial fate!

Rather than pursuing a volatile career path with no sustainable reward for delivering an outstanding professional performance, he asked himself how he could prevent this situation from happening again.

The resolution came quickly as he sought to answer one gigantic question: Why is he here on this earth—what is his purpose?

He picked up the book entitled *Action Strategies for Personal Achievement* by Brian Tracy, and it was a major home run! Although there are countless jewels in this book, the two golden nuggets that paved the path to discovering his purpose were as follows:

First, he learned his purpose was wrapped in his best gifts and talents; that's what he was born to give to this world. If you do not know your best gifts and talents, ask fifteen people who know you well. The people he asked unanimously said his gifts were found in guiding, directing, and leading others. Can you say wow? Jesse learned this truth when those fifteen people pointed that out.

Second, Brian Tracy said that if you read an hour a day in your field of study, you could become an expert in that field in five years. Jesse couldn't speak about where Mr. Tracy found evidence to support his statement, but he trusted him. It gave Jesse great joy to know that he could shift from a long career in hospitality to a new vocation in personal and professional development as a success coach and inspirational speaker.

## *"Change Your Thinking, Change Your Life." – Brian Tracy*

93

**Are you ready to explore new resources and perspectives that could transform your thinking and ignite a positive change in your life? Yes___ No___**

**To help you prepare for a positive life transformation, do our Best Gifts & Talents exercise below; we also refer to this as Purpose Gifts & Talents (PGT):**

1. Contact your network: Find ten people who know you well, such as close friends, family members, colleagues, or mentors.

2. Ask for honest feedback: Request that they share what they believe are your best gifts and talents.

3. Compile the responses: Write down the gifts and talents they mention.

4. Identify Common Themes: Look for patterns or common themes in their feedback to identify your most recognized strengths.

5. Reflect on the feedback: Consider how these strengths align with your personal goals and how they can help you in your journey toward a positive life transformation.

This exercise gives you valuable insights into your unique abilities and how others perceive your strengths. This can be very empowering and guiding as you embark on a new chapter in your life.

*"It's All About How You Leave Them Feeling"*
*– Jesse Ferrell*

# Best Gifts & Talents Feedback

# Best Gifts & Talents Feedback

**Use your imagination to draw what this future looks like for you and your family below:**

# AAA Life Strategy Concept

Dealing with newly discovered, unavoidable life difficulties can be crippling. Sometimes, you may not know where to look for solutions to settle complex problems. We will call times like this a global crisis. While writing *How You Leave Them Feeling: Your Foundation for Inspiring Relationships*, we experienced COVID-19, which we viewed as a global crisis.

The best answer for meaningful solutions to this problem was invented in a fifteen-minute conversation between Jesse and Lisa. They called this solution their **AAA Life Strategy.**

The first *A* in this life strategy concept stands for *Attitude.* Take a close look at your attitude and determine your ongoing disposition relative to how you feel about the difficulties and unknown effects this global crisis (or any other crisis) has on you and those you love and care about.

Your attitude is what either attracts or repels people. They either want to connect with you or run for the hills to get away from you if you have a negative attitude. If you have a glowing and attractive attitude, people will appreciate you. From our experience, it is not a common trait. Use your attractive glow to connect with and infuse your positive energy and vibration into the lives of others.

The second powerful *A* in our life strategy concept is *Adjust.* Don't settle for merely surviving difficult things. Be clear on what adjustments you need to make to thrive, even when the world seems to be falling apart.

You might say this is easier said than done, but what we say is...if not said, likely not done! Consider using your best creativity to connect with other positive people to help you create a pleasing life by any positive means necessary. Be sure you make any adjustments necessary to sustain a pleasing attitude.

The final powerful *A* in our life strategy concept is *Adapt.* Make sure you are willing and able to adapt a forward-thinking life strategy that brings together a consistently positive attitude following your prudent adjustments. Choose to continue rising again...again, and again!

Live by the expression, "You are either up or getting up!" Use our AAA life strategy Whenever you slip down a pattern of darkness, and it feels like life is getting the best of you. Highlight that it's designed to simplify whatever you feel is complex.

Adhering to our AAA Life Strategy Concept can create a positive turnaround in the right direction, leaving you feeling relieved and reassured! To enroll our AAA Life Strategy Concept into your life, answer the questions below:

1. **What is my current attitude about work and life matters?**

_____

_____

_____

_____

_____

_____

2. **What must I adjust to fully align with my values and chosen roles so I can live my best life now?**

_____

_____

_____

_____

_____

3. **Regarding the AAA Life Strategy concept, what must I do to adapt to my chosen adjustments?**

_____

_____

_____

_____

## "Your Attitude, Not Your Aptitude, Will Determine Your Altitude" – Zig Ziglar

## Not Starting All Over

Another concept we use when coaching individuals is *"Starting over, not starting ALL OVER again."* This can provide a new way to view problems and potentially transform a crisis into a more manageable situation.

Choosing to *"start over"* rather than *"start ALL OVER again"* is based on a simple reversal of perspective.

Implementing the practice of 'starting over, not starting all over again' is an effective method for dealing with the need to transform a personal crisis. It also represents the new *GRASP* concept in action. By shifting your perspective from commonplace to extraordinary, you can start *living your life by design*.

For a deeper understanding and the full story, go to page 119 in our book, *How You Leave Them Feeling: Your Foundation for Relationships*.

**Following your review of page 119, as noted above, how might adopting the mindset of "starting over, not starting all over again" help you reframe a crisis and find a more manageable path forward? Write your strategy below:**

**My Starting Over Strategy**

_____

_____

_____

_____

_____

_____

_____

*"New Beginnings Are Often Described as Painful Endings" -Lau Tzu*

We have designed a system to help you gain more clarity when you are stuck figuring out difficult life matters. Often, these situations can feel like a crisis without a clear and obvious "right" choice. For example, you may be deciding whether or not to quit your current job and move to a job that (you hope) will bring you more value. Another example would be deciding between two real estate companies when searching for the right place to hang your real estate license.

We believe using a pros and cons rating scale will help you think on paper.

On the following page, make a detailed list of your pros and cons related to whatever crisis you are managing or decision you are trying to make. List and rate the essential facts of concern for each company. Use a 10-point scale, whereby 1 represents a shallow perceivable value and 10 represents the highest value.

Once you have totaled your ratings, examine the overall score for the two choices and determine if the choice with the higher quality rating is the best decision. This process allows you to remove the conflict or what feels like a crisis to make the best choice.

# Crisis Management Pros & Cons Rating Scale

| | Facts of Concern | Pros & Cons | | Facts of Concern | Pros & Cons | | Point Variance |
|---|---|---|---|---|---|---|---|
| 1 | | | | | | | |
| 2 | | | | | | | |
| 3 | | | | | | | |
| 4 | | | | | | | |
| 5 | | | | | | | |
| 6 | | | | | | | |
| 7 | | | | | | | |
| 8 | | | | | | | |
| 9 | | | | | | | |
| 10 | | | | | | | |
| 11 | | | | | | | |
| 12 | | | | | | | |
| 13 | | | | | | | |
| 14 | | | | | | | |
| 15 | | | | | | | |

Total Point Variance

| Crisis Management Pros & Cons Rating Scale |
|---|
| 0 = very low perceivable value |
| 10 = highest perceivable value |

The following page contains a sample rating system for choosing to work for Century 21 and Keller Williams brokers.

Century 21 has a total of 7.3 on a 10-point scale, and Keller Williams Realty has a capacity of 5.2 on the same 10-point scale.

This comparison represents a 2-point favor for Century 21. Using this Crisis Management Pros & Cons tool can help lend weight to making a prudent choice of real estate brokers.

# Keller Williams Realty Crisis Management Pros & Cons Rating Scale

| | Facts of Concern | Century 21 Pros & Cons | | Facts of Concern | Keller Williams Realty Pros & Cons | Point Variance |
|---|---|---|---|---|---|---|
| 1 | 7 | Downtown location | | 4 | Keller Williams Realty Location | -3 |
| 2 | 9 | Luxury listing value | | 5 | Luxury listing value | -4 |
| 3 | 6 | Commissions | | 9 | Commissions | 3 |
| 4 | 8 | Fees | | 6 | Fees | -2 |
| 5 | 7 | Leads | | 4 | Leads | -3 |
| 6 | 7 | Marketing expenses | | 3 | Marketing expenses | -4 |
| 7 | 8 | Transition factor | | 5 | Transition factor | -3 |
| 8 | 8 | Broker quality | | 7 | Broker quality | -1 |
| 9 | 8 | Development opportunity | | 5 | Development opportunity | -3 |
| 10 | 6 | Autonomy | | 8 | Autonomy | 2 |
| 11 | 9 | Signing bonus | | 0 | Signing bonus | -9 |
| 12 | 8 | Access to key personnel | | 9 | Access to key personnel | 1 |
| 13 | 9 | Benefits package (referrals agent) | | 4 | Benefits package (referrals agent) | -5 |
| 14 | 7 | Compensation package | | 5 | Compensation package | -2 |
| 15 | 8 | Customer factor (quality and quantity of customers) | | 6 | Customer factor (quality and quantity of customers) | -2 |
| 16 | 4 | Professional expectations | | 6 | Professional expectations | 2 |
| 17 | 5 | Freedom factor - freedom for getting job done | | 8 | Freedom factor - freedom for getting job done | 3 |
| 18 | 9 | Future longevity (how long can it remain like this) | | 6 | Future longevity (how long can it remain like this) | -3 |
| 19 | 8 | Lifestyle affected | | 4 | Lifestyle affected | -4 |
| 20 | 7 | Their management style | | 7 | Their management style | 0 |
| 21 | 7 | Reputation, integrity and delivering as promised | | 5 | Reputation, integrity and delivering as promised | -2 |
| 22 | 6 | Stress level and pressure | | 6 | Stress level and pressure | 0 |
| 23 | 5 | Team fair play occupational hazard and people Factor | | 4 | Team fair play occupational hazard and people Factor | -1 |
| 24 | 8 | Work environment and company culture | | 5 | Work environment and company culture | -3 |

| 7.3 |
|---|

| 5.2 |
|---|

| Century 21 | Keller Williams Realty | Total Point Variance |
|---|---|---|
| 7.3 | 5.2 | 2.01 |

| Crisis Management Pros & Cons Rating Scale |
|---|
| 0 = very low perceivable value |
| 10 = highest perceivable value |

# NOTES

*"Nothing Will Work Unless You Do" – Maya Angelou*

# NOTES

*"If You Fail to Plan, You Are Planning to Fail" – Benjamin Franklin*

# CHAPTER 11

# Work and Love — It's All in the Balance

We have encountered many dedicated professionals who struggle to balance the hours they spend on their professional and personal relationships. While those relationships may intertwine at various points, you'll discover immense value in learning to manage these two pillars separately yet with mutual respect.

When engaging others in personal or professional collaborations, ensure the timing suits all parties. Don't assume that just because you feel it is crucial and the timing is right for you, it is also suitable for others.

When respecting the "time and timing" concept, we use one of our business rules to help govern our time. Our business operating hours are from 6 a.m. to 6 p.m. Outside of those hours, we put our work down.

When we accept emergency client calls after 6 p.m., we make it a point to take them outside our home office work areas. This practice preserves the positive energy of our home, allowing us to keep work stress from seeping into our personal space.

Following this rule, we ensure the other partner can relax without feeling trapped in a high-pressure work environment. We both value this arrangement because it helps us maintain a sense of control and respect in our lives, making our work more manageable and our home a place of peace.

Even if you aren't choosing to design business rules to help you manage work and life, know this: work and love are all in the balance. You've heard it more than once: *It's All About How You Leave Them Feeling!* This also includes how you leave yourself feeling.

Consider the following guiding principles related to your work environment, allowing you to embrace a roadmap for success while leaving yourself and others feeling great.

## Guiding Principles for Work and Relationships

1. Determine your most productive hours for excelling in your professional space.

2. Take periodic breaks for at least five minutes following an hour of total concentration.

3. Determine a work schedule that allows you to serve with total commitment.

4. After completing your work commitment, put down all professional concerns.

5. Build love, creativity, and organic sharing within your meaningful relationships.

Answer the following questions to establish the best guiding principles for your work and important relationships:

**1. Determine which hours you are most productive in your professional space.**

_____

_____

_____

_____

_____

_____

_____

_____

_____

*"If you have a strong purpose in life, you don't have to be pushed. Your passion will drive you there." – Roy T. Bennett*

2. You will benefit from taking periodic breaks of at least five minutes after every hour of focused work. Below, you'll find suggestions for different break activities. Circle the options you like:

    1. Take a short walk around the block

    2. Sit still and doing nothing

    3. Lay on your bed or sofa and close your eyes

    4. Listen to music

    5. Engage in quiet or guided meditation

If none of the choices above work for you, list three activities below that you will do on your five-minute breaks following each hour of focus:

_____

_____

_____

_____

_____

_____

3. What does it look like for you to create a work schedule that enables you to serve with complete commitment?

_____

_____

_____

_____

_____

_____

_____

1. Share why setting aside all professional concerns once you've fulfilled your work commitments is beneficial.

_____

_____

_____

_____

_____

_____

_____

_____

_____

_____

2. How can fostering creativity and organic sharing enrich your most important relationships?

_____

_____

_____

_____

_____

_____

_____

## CHAPTER 12

# Conclusion: How Do You Leave People Feeling?

We encourage you to apply these principles and answer one major question: How Do You Leave People Feeling?

We trust that you have found nuggets of value throughout this book. We live in unique and uncertain times. Countless people are suffering and are hungry for positive, meaningful relationships.

*How You Leave Them Feeling: Your Foundation for Inspiring Relationships* is foundational. It allows you to gain value in your life by simply leaving everyone you meet and everything you touch better than you found them.

Applying the principles from this book is not a complex task. Just by understanding the concept and making a conscious effort, you can start your journey toward greatness. Here are a few of our favorite principles from our book to get you started:

## The Umuntu Factor
## Turning a Crisis Into Abundance
## Living Life by Design

Although we practice the full breadth of the concepts noted in this book, we focus on the top three concepts and chapters stated above. Your final exercise is to choose your top three favorite chapters and share below why they resonated with you:

1. **My first favorite chapter is** _____
   **Why this chapter is important to me is:**

   _____

   _____

   _____

   _____

   _____

   _____

   _____

2. **My second favorite chapter is** _____
   **Why this chapter is important to me is:**

   _____

   _____

   _____

   _____

   _____

   _____

   _____

**3. My third favorite chapter is** _____
   **Why this chapter is important to me is:**

_____

_____

_____

_____

_____

_____

_____

By signing my name below, I'm committing to enrolling my top three favorite chapters into my life!

_____        _____
          My Signature                              Date

_____        _____
    Accountability Partner Name                     Date

# How You Leave Them Feeling Appreciation

The 'How You Leave Them Feeling' concept is not just a foundational idea; it's a transformative power. It empowers you to enrich your life by simply leaving a positive impact on everyone you meet and everything you touch. By embracing this concept, you are already on the path to greatness.

We trust our interactive companion workbook inspired you to live by design rather than happenstance. Per your signature, you have agreed to remain committed to the work. We ask that you immediately start applying your favorite principles, recommendations, or lessons learned from the work featured in this workbook.

## Lisa & Jesse Workbook Completion Gratitude Video

A heartfelt thank you to Sheryl Green, our dedicated development, content, and grammatical editor. Her expertise and meticulous attention to detail have been invaluable in creating an exceptional educational experience for our readers.

# Testimonials

What a beautiful collaboration of work from Jesse and Lisa! I was left "feeling good" after finishing their book. There are so many words of wisdom that you can put into action and apply right away. Because so many people don't realize how deeply they can impact those around them, the simple (but not always easy) concept of leaving situations better than you found them and leaving others wanting more of your presence is a concept that anyone could stand to incorporate more into their lives.

You'll find a vast array of guidelines in their book dealing with relationships of all kinds, and life in general to up-level how you choose to live it. Thank you for sharing this valuable information and always being a model of what you teach! **Lisa Ulshafer**

I am highly impressed. The book emphasizes the importance of being mindful and intentional in our lives and encourages readers to take the time to live life rather than exist. Jesse and Lisa provide practical tools and advice on implementing intention into our daily lives, and their writings are both inspiring and thought-provoking. I highly recommend this book as it will help readers to be more mindful and intentional and ultimately live by design. I hope this work takes off and finds itself on every nightstand in the nation! **Edin Olano**

If you would like to work with JessTalk and LisaListen **scan the QR code below** to share information about you or your company and book a 30-minute conference call. We look forward to connecting with you soon!

**Contact Us**

**JessTalk Website**

**How You Leave Them Feeling
Your Foundation for
Inspiring Relationships**

**Yellow Audiobook**

**How You Leave Them Feeling
Your Foundation for
Inspiring Relationships**

**Yellow Hardcover Book**

# How You Leave Them Feeling
## The Ultimate Key for Personal & Professional Success Second Edition

### Blue Hardcover Book